Death Anxiety among Students:
A Case Study of Manipur University

Rajkumar Suresh Singh

(M.A., M.Ed., UGC-NET in Education and Adult Education)

CANADIAN
Academic Publishing

2014

Price : $27.86

First Edition : 2014

ISBN : 978-0-9921651-9-2

Publisher ISBN Prefix : 978-0-9921651

ISBN Allotment Agency : Library and Archives Canada (Govt. of Canada)

Published & Printed by

Canadian Academic Publishing
81, Woodlot Crescent,
Etobicoke,
Toronto, Ontario, Canada.
Postal Code- M9W 6T3
Phone- +1 (647) 633 9712
http://www.canadapublish.com

Contents

Contents

CHAPTER – 1

INTRODUCTION

It has been the practice to treat death anxiety as a uniform or single entity, without recognizing the underlying typology. The importance of refining that concept comes from clinical findings that different types of traumatic events lead to different forms of death anxiety, each of which is experienced and responded to by humans in a distinctive manner. These responses are both conscious and unconscious i.e. within or outside direct awareness. The former are generally well known and these include traumatic and post-traumatic stress syndromes and responses to cancer and other types of grave illness. But it is not generally appreciated that death anxiety is prompted by every type of traumatic event and that it can register and operate entirely outside of awareness. The effects, nonetheless, are powerful and often devastating, and always include a tightening of communication defenses in an effect to obliterate the conscious recognition of the various ways that a given trauma is imparting on the individual and the extent to which death-related anxieties have been activated.

1.1 DEATH ANXIETY

Death anxiety refers to the fear and apprehension of one's own death. It is the neurotic fear of loss of the self which in intense state parallels feelings of helplessness and depression. Man's awareness of his own death produces anxiety that can only be dealt with by recognizing one's individuality. Man's awareness of death gives him the responsibility of finding meaning in life.

Death is a biological, personal, socio-cultural and existential phenomenon.[1] Knowledge of people's concerns and fears regarding death and dying has important theoretical and practical implications in addressing issues around end-of-life care.[2] The biological death is useful to distinguish between the process of aging and the ending called death. Yet when the

1

actual time comes, and the individual faces death alone, the psychological reactions appear to be remarkably similar.

Elizabeth Kübler-Ross found that in the majority of persons, almost regardless of age, the personal reactions to imminent death pass through five phases- Denial, Anger, Bargaining, Depression and Acceptance (although not every individual achieves the final phase). Dying and death, like other major aspects of human life, are also very important cultural and social phenomena.[3]

The death can be fully understood only if it is viewed as one of the central meanings of human existence. An idea of the centrality of one's own death can be gathered if individuals could be made to contemplate seriously the possibility of their own death.[4]

As death is the final stage of life cycle, it can be approached naturally by dying individuals and their families. Death and dying can be seen as a part of life process, or they can be viewed as a dramatic, painful, tortured experience both for the individual and the families. Increasingly, more research reports are being presented on the nature of death and dying. Research on exactly when death occurs, how the dying should be treated, and how their families might better cope will continue for many years.[5]

Even though death most commonly occurs in later years, it may happen at any stage of life. Accidents and suicides are the major causes of death among younger persons, and continue to be so in later years, although their relative significance declines. Often death is associated with some special psychological stress, it may be acute mourning, or an anniversary, or some particular loss of status or self-esteem.

Death is sometimes defined as the absence of certain clinically detectable vital signs. More recently, death has sometimes been defined as the lack of brain wave activity. Still other says that death can only be defined as a bodily state which represents an irreversible loss of vital functions and from which the individual cannot possibly be retrieved. According to the concept of terminal drop, death can be predicted from certain dramatic changes in cognitive function in the period preceding demise, i.e., significant changes both in personal adjustment and performance may serve as indicators of impeding death.[6]

The meaning of life and death vary from one individual to another.[7] The act of dying itself may involve a certain amount of "anticipatory self grief", grief over the loss of one's own life- that, fears what it may be to lose one's self. In addition, fear of dying is often associated with unfounded beliefs that dying itself is quite painful, that one may be abandoned by everyone when dying, that death involves an ultimate aloneness, and "that there may be final medical procedure that will further dehumanize oneself by being turned into a sort of plumbing shop..."[8]

The fear of pain can be relieved by the knowledge of modern pain relieving processes. It can help to know that though dying is rarely pleasant, it is neither as painful nor as unpleasant as is often feared. Fear of dying involves not only physiological but psychological factors, too. Pain is more easily dealt with than loneliness.

Robert Langs[9] identified three classes of death anxiety-

1. *Predatory Death Anxiety*: This form is the oldest phylogenetically in the cellular organisms which have receptors that have evolved to react to external dangers and they also possess self-protective, responsive mechanisms designed to insure survival in the face of chemical and physical forms of attack or danger. In humans, this form of death anxiety is evolved by a variety of dangerous situations that put the recipient at risk or threatens his or her survival. These traumas may be psychological and/or physical. Predatory death anxieties mobilizes an individual's adaptive resource and lead to fight or flight, active efforts to combat the danger or attempts to escape the threatening situation. These responses also may take mental and/or

physical forms, and include both conscious and unconscious processing and modes of adapting.

2. *Predation Death Anxiety:* This form of death anxiety arises when an individual harms others physically and/or mentally. The arousal of this type of anxiety often involves unconscious rather than conscious realizations and processing. The primary reaction to this type of anxiety is that of conscious and unconscious guilt, which, in turn, motivates a variety of self-punitive decisions and actions by the perpetrator of harm to others whose deeper sources go unappreciated.

3. *Existential Death Anxiety:* This is the most powerful form of death anxiety and its activation is based in humans on the definitive, conscious awareness and anticipation of the inevitability of personal demise. This expectation and the anxieties it evokes are the result of human language awareness of the distinction of personal identity, and the ability to anticipate the future. Humans defended against this type of death anxiety through denial, which is effected through a wide range of mental mechanisms and physical actions, which may also go unrecognized. While limited use of denial tends to be adaptive, its use is usually excessive and proves to be costly emotionally.

Although humans have always thought about death, empirical research on death anxiety didn't begin in earnest until the late 1950s.[10] The fear of death has been rated as the most common and the second worst fear that troubles us.[11] Many are traumatized long before they near their end from their impending death. Many suffer from death anxiety but are able to function.

Death anxiety is defined as an abnormally great fear of death, with feelings of dread or apprehension arising when one thinks about the process of dying or what happens after death.[12] Longman Dictionary of Psychology and Psychiatry defines death anxiety as "a depressive state in which anxiety over dying and fear of death (thanatophobia) are salient symptoms".[13] Death anxiety has been defined as "a point of view of dying, a part of the fabric of being the child develops before a precise conceptual formulation, that is, it exists prior to and outside of language and image".[14]

1.2 STATEMENT OF THE PRESENT PROBLEM

The study explores the degree of death anxiety among students undergoing post-graduate courses in Manipur University. Further attempt was also made to find out the difference in death anxiety according to sex.

1.3 RATIONALE OF THE STUDY

Since ancient times, human beings have searched for the *'Fountain of Youth'*- some means prolonged youth, and life, indefinitely. But alas, such dreams have remained only illusions; while life and health can be prolonged through proper diet, exercise and reduced exposure to various sources of stress, there appears to be no way to live forever.

Death is the inevitable end of life. Changing environment, conflicts and dreaded diseases has been the one of the causes of death anxiety all over the world. News of murder, bomb-attacks, death, especially 'bullet-deaths', has become a "regular news item" of the local dailies. In a conflict situation prevailing in the state, the environment for education has become polluted.

Manipur, a small State in the North-Eastern India, is better known in the world to-day as a strife-torn place. Though populated only by 22, 93, 896 persons as per the Census of India, 2001, [15] Manipur is within 36 areas of conflict zones of the world.[16]

Approximately 30 (thirty) armed groups (non-state actors) were reported to be operating in and around the State.[17] Demands for sovereignty and homeland were the basic objectives of these armed groups. As a result, the entire State has been in turmoil for the last five decades. In order to tackle the armed activities and to assist the civil administration, the whole State was declared as 'Disturbed Area' on September 8, 1980.

In the recent past, Manipur experienced major upheavals or social drama and the educational institutions remained 'closed' for more than four months. Such situations/conditions cater to creation of imbalances in the society. Almost every person in Manipur has death-related experiences in one way or the other.

Death related trauma may lead to constructive actions, more often than not; they lead to actions that are, in the short or long run, damaging of self or others. The present study attempts to study the death anxiety among post-graduate students. The study is felt significant by the researcher because at the time of stress, and especially when the scepter of death anxiety has been activated, it is important to be on the alert for decisions and actions that are unconsciously motivated by the need to deny death because they almost prove exceedingly costly for all concerned. In such conflict situation education is always at stake.

The findings may be of practical value to the planners and policy makers in providing the necessary feedback to the student community reading in the highest educational institution.

1.4 OBJECTIVES OF THE STUDY

The objectives of the present study were:

(i) To study the death anxiety among post-graduate students.

(ii) To find out the difference in death anxiety between male and female students.

(iii) To suggest remedial measures for improving the existing situation.

1.5 DELIMITATIONS OF THE STUDY

The study was confined to the death anxiety and to the examination of the difference in death anxiety between male and female students of Manipur University.

1.6   OPERATIONAL DEFINITIONS OF KEY TERMS

DEATH:

According to Dictionary of Behavioral Science, death is "cessation of bodily and mental functions vital to the organism".[18]

Stedman's Medical Dictionary defines death as "1. the cessation of life, 2. in multi-cellular organisms, death is a gradual process at the cellular level, with tissues varying in their ability to withstand deprivation of oxygen. In higher organisms, death is a cessation of integrated tissue and organic functions. 3. In man, death is manifested by the loss of heart beat, by the absence of spontaneous breathing, and by cerebral death".[19]

Collins Standard Dictionary defines death as "1. the act of fact of dying; final ending of life".[20]

Death has been defined in Longman Dictionary of Psychology and Psychiatry as "technically, the cessation of physical and mental processes in an organism, sometimes determined in humans by two flap encephalograph readings taken 24 hours apart. Death may signify the end of the patient's life in a particular environment as a step forward rebirth in another, without actual cessation of physical or mental functions".[21]

Encarta World English Dictionary defines death as "1. cessation of physical life, 2. extinction of anything; destruction, 3. something likely to produce death, a cause or occasion of death, 4. something considered terrible as death, 5. the cessation, absence or opposite of spiritual life, spiritual and eternal ruin, 6. a fatal plague, 7. a personification, type, or representation of mortality, generally a skeleton holding a scythe, 8. slaughter, bloodshed, 9. the condition of being death".[22]

The New International Webster's Dictionary and Thesaurus of the English Language defines death as "1. end of being alive, the ending of all vital functions or processes in an organism or cell, 2. a way of dying, 3. an instance of somebody's dying, 4. the condition or quality of being death." **[23]**

ANXIETY:

Anxiety is a "specific state of unpleasure accompanied by motor discharge along definite pathways." [24]

"The ego's reaction to external threats is called fear. When the ego is exposed to threats from within, that is, coming from the id or the superego, its reaction to such a threat is called anxiety." [25]

According to H.S. Sullivan, "Anxiety results whenever the biological needs of an individual cannot be satisfied in a socially acceptable way. The individual develops a feeling of insecurity and uneasiness. It is always connected with an increased muscle tension. Muscles ready for a socially unacceptable action become inhibited since their activity is likely to invite disapproval. Anxiety is a socially produced muscular tension which interferes with other tensions or normal mental functioning." [26]

According to K. Horney, anxiety is "a feeling of loneliness and helplessness toward a potential hostile world." [27]

Stedman's Medical Dictionary defines anxiety as "1. in psychoanalysis, apprehension of danger and dread accompanied by restlessness, tension, tachycardia, and dyspnea unattached to a clearly identifiable stimulus, 2. in experimental psychology, a drive or motivational state learned from previously neutral cues." [28]

Collins Standard Dictionary defines anxiety as "1. a state of being uneasy or worried about what may happen, 2. an eager but often uneasy desire." [29]

Longman Dictionary of Psychology and Psychiatry defines anxiety as "a preservative feeling of dread, apprehension, and impending disaster." [30]

Anxiety should be distinguished from fear. Fear is a response to a clear and present danger; anxiety is a response to an undefined or unknown threat which in many cases stems from unconscious conflicts, feelings of insecurity, or forbidden impulses within us. In both, however, the body mobilizes itself to meet the threat, and muscles become tense, breathing is faster, and the heart beats more rapidly.

Encarta World English Dictionary defines anxiety as "1. feeling of worry, nervousness or agitation, often about something that is going to happen, 2. a subject or concern that causes worry, 3. the strong wish to do a particular thing, especially if the wish is unnecessarily or unhealthy strong, 4. a state of abnormal and intense apprehension or fear of real or imagined danger, manifested psychologically as increased heart rate, sweating, trembling, weakness, and stomach or intestinal discomfort".[31]

The New International Webster's Dictionary and Thesaurus of the English Language defines anxiety as "1. disturbance of mind regarding some uncertain events, misgiving worry, 2. strained or solicitous desire, as for some object or purpose, eagerness".[32]

DEATH ANXIETY

Death anxiety is a depressive state in which anxiety over dying and fear of death are the salient symptoms.

POST-GRADUATE STUDENTS

Post-Graduate as pointed out in the Webster's New World Dictionary: "for taking a course of study after graduation", "a student taking such courses". For the purpose of this study, Post-Graduate is taken as "the student taking a course of study after graduation under 10+2+3 systems as practiced in India".

1.7 HYPOTHESES OF THE STUDY

(i)   The death anxiety is high among University students.

(ii)   There is no significant difference in death anxiety between male and female students.

9

REFERENCES

[1] Robert A. Baron. (2001). Psychology, 3rd ed., New Delhi: Prentice Hall of India Private Limited, p.366.

[2] Catherine So-Kum Tang; Anise M.S. Wu; and Elise C.W. Yan. (2002). Psychosocial Correlates of Death Anxiety among Chinese College Students. *Death Studies*, 26:p.491-499.

[3] Elizabeth Kübler-Ross. (1969). On Death and Dying. New York: Macmillan.

[4] J. B. McCarthy. (1980). Death Anxiety: The Loss of Self. USA: Gardner.

[5] L. A. Lefton. (1982). Psychology, 2nd ed., USA: Allyn and Bacon.

[6] K. F. Reigal and R. M. Reigal. (1972). Development, drop and death. *Development Psychology*, 6:p.306-319.

[7] Elizabeth Kübler-Ross. (1975). Death: The final stages of growth. New Jersey: Prentice Hall.

[8] R. N. Holocomb. (1975). Why Survive? Being Old in America. New York: Harper and Row.

[9] Robert Langs. (1997). Death Anxiety and Clinical Practice. London: Karnac Books.

[10] Joseph A. Dulark. (2002). Encyclopedia of Aging. New York: Quill.

[11] Anubhutti Rattan. (2005). the Question of Death and Death Anxiety, New York: Simon and Schuster.

[12] Webster's Dictionary (1980). Canada: Trident Press International.

[13] Longman Dictionary of Psychology and Psychiatry (1984). New York: Longman.

[14] Mary Ireland. (1993). Death Anxiety and Self-Esteem in Children Four, Five and Six Years of Age: a Comparison of Minority Children who have AIDS with Minority Children who are healthy (Four-year-old, Five-year-old, Six-year-old Immune Deficiency). *Dissertation Abstracts International*, Vol. 56-01, Section: B, p.0172.

[15] Statistical Abstract Manipur. (2005). Directorate of Economics and Statistics, Government of Manipur.

[16] Uppsala Conflict Data Programme (UCDP). (2008). International Data Base. http://www.ucdp.uu.se/. Accessed on March 15, 2010.

[17] Col. Ved Prakash. (2008). Terrorism in India's North East: A Gathering Strom. Delhi: Kalpaz Publication. Vol. I & II.

[18] Dictionary of Behavioral Science. (1973). New York: Van Nostrand Reinhold Company.

[19] Stedman's Medical Dictionary. 23rd ed. (1976). USA: The Williams and Wilkins Company.

[20] Collins Standard Dictionary. (1978). New Delhi: Oxford and IBH Publishing Co.

[21] Longman Dictionary of Psychology and Psychiatry. (1984). New York: Longman.

[22] Encarta World English Dictionary. (1999). Sydney: Pan Macmillan Australia Private Limited.

[23] The New International Webster's Dictionary and Thesaurus of the English Language (International Encyclopedic Edition). (2002). Canada: Trident Press International.

[24] Sigmund Freud. (1926). In Dictionary of Behavioral Science. Op. Cit. p.27.

[25] Sigmund Freud. (1932). New Introductory Lectures on Psycho-Analysis, tr. By Sprott, W.J.H., Norton, New York, 1933. p.53.

[26] Sullivan, H. S. In Dictionary of Behavioral Science. Op. Cit. p.28.

[27] K. Horney. (1937). In Dictionary of Behavioral Science. Ibid.

[28] Stedman's Medical Dictionary. Op. Cit.

[29] Collins Standard Dictionary. (1978). Op. Cit.

[30] Longman Dictionary of Psychology and Psychiatry. (1984). Op. Cit.

[31] Encarta World English Dictionary. (1999).Op. Cit.

[32] The New International Webster's Dictionary and Thesaurus of the English Language (International Encyclopedic Edition). (2002).Op. Cit.

CHAPTER – 2
REVIEW OF RELATED LITERATURE

An essential and crucial aspect of a research project is the review of literature. It is a serious step of research which includes a review of related literature more extensively. So, it is most essential for a research worker to be well informed about both the specific problem under investigation and related studies. The reviews of related literature gives an insight into the problem and help the investigator to acquaint himself with the techniques and methodology followed by earlier investigator to find an answer to the problem under investigation. Survey of related literature means to locate, to read and to evaluate the past as well as current literature of the research concerned with the planned investigation.

2.1   IMPORTANCE OF REVIEW OF RELATED LITERATURE

About the importance of review of related literature, Samuel has written the praise worthy statement, "With correct sense of mind, the importance of related literature can't be denied in any research. Though it is time-consuming, it is fruitful phase of any scientific investigation. The main purpose is to systematically portray the relevant aspects of the study into theoretical frameworks".

According to John W. Best, "Practically all human knowledge can be found in books and libraries. Unlike other animals that must start anew with each generation, man builds upon the accumulated and recorded knowledge of the past. His consistent adding to the vast store of knowledge makes possible progress in all areas of human endeavor".

Review of related studies avoid the risk of duplication, provides theories, ideas, explanations or hypothesis valuable in formulating the problem and contribute to the general scholarship of the investigator. A familiarity with the literature in any problem helps the investigator to discover what is already known, what others have attempted to find out, what method of attack have been promising or disappointing and what problem remains to be solved.

Review of related literature allows the researcher to acquaint himself with current knowledge in the field in which he is going to conduct his research. Besides this, it enables the researcher to define and delimit his problem. It helps the researcher in searching those areas in which positive findings are likely to result and his endeavors would be likely to add to the knowledge in a meaningful way. It also gives the researcher an understanding of the research methodology, way of study, knowledge about the tools and instruments etc.

Emphasizing the importance of survey of related literature, C. V. Good and others have clearly pointed out that "Survey of related literature helps us to know whether evidences already available can solve problems adequately without duplication". It may suggest that findings, the way in which studies are comparable and in which they are related to one another. On the basis, it seems safe to conclude that a review of related literature in any area of investigation is of paramount significance.

The present review is by no means complete or exhaustive. It is an attempt to indicate the main trends of research in this specific area which have a direct or indirect bearing on the present problem. In the present study, it has not been possible on the part of the investigator, due to lack of resources and time, to get access into the entire fold of published and unpublished research in the field, yet an attempt is made to view a few such information of the problem at hand as well as references, books, monographs and research conducted in the field, educational abstracts and journals, etc. In order to seek some guidelines from the earlier studies in this specific area of research, the findings of some relevant and representative studies are discussed in the subsequent pages. For the sake of convenience, the investigator has divided the related studies in two parts:

(i)   Studies Conducted Abroad.
(ii)   Studies in India.

2.2 STUDIES CONDUCTED ABROAD

Koocher, G. P., et al., (1976)[1] conducted a study on "Death anxiety in normal children and adolescents". Instruments devised to measure death anxiety, depression, and manifest anxiety in adults were administered to 75 junior high-school students, 111 senior high-school students, and 38 adults in an effort to determine the nature of any developmental differences among these groups. A number of significant differences were noted, with the senior high-school students showing greater anxiety, depression, and death anxiety than the other groups. These results are discussed in the context of tasks of adolescent development, and an item analysis of the death anxiety questionnaire is presented.

Tate, L. A., (1982)[2] studied "Life satisfaction and death anxiety in aged women". The life satisfaction and death anxiety of elderly women were investigated as a function of demographic, life history, and stress variables. Through multiple regression, life satisfaction was predicted by number of friends, good health, and, surprisingly, by having fewer offspring living in the same city. Health problems, change in living conditions, and relatively high educational level were predictors of death anxiety. It was concluded that life satisfaction and death anxiety are a function of past and present life experiences and conditions.

Lee P.W., et al., (1983-1984)[3] conducted a study on "Death anxiety in leukemic Chinese children". The pattern of psychopathology in Chinese leukemic children as compared to Chinese children with orthopedic disorder was studied through analysis of their respective responses to the Children's Apperception Test. Leukemic children were found to exhibit a distinctly different pattern of psychopathology and psychological defenses. Isolation, detachment and denial were commonly used to defend against their insecurity, abstract fears and uncertainties. Themes relating to parental misunderstandings and maltreatment were also elicited. These findings are discussed in relation to the Chinese conception of death as a taboo subject. Recommendations are made for a better psychological management of fatally ill children and their parents.

14

Niemeyer, R. A., and Niemeyer, G. J., (1984)[4] conducted a study on "'Death anxiety and counseling skill in the suicide interventionist". It was hypothesized that suicide intervention workers may experience greater fear of death than the general population. The study examined the death anxiety of interventionists and its relation to skill in responding to suicidal clients. A sample of 109 suicide prevention workers from three independent crisis centers were administered the Death Anxiety Scale (Templer, 1970) and the Suicide Intervention Response Inventory (Niemeyer & MacInnes, 1981).

Compared to 109 matched controls, the interventionists were found to have significantly lower death anxiety, thereby reversing the earlier finding. Moreover, no linear or curvilinear relationship between death anxiety and suicide counseling skill could be identified. Together, these results give some justification to the traditional neglect of death concern as a factor in screening or training crisis intervention personnel.

Mahabeer, M., and Bhana, K. (1984)[5] studied "The relationship between religion, religiosity and death anxiety among Indian adolescents" among Indian university and high school students living in South Africa and representing in equal numbers the Christian, Hindu and Muslim faith and examined the influence of age, sex and religion and the relationship between death anxiety and religiosity. Equal numbers of male and female subjects were included in each age and religious group. Results showed that Muslims subjects were more death anxious than Christian or Hindu subjects. The degree of commitment to religious practices and beliefs did not intensify or reduce death anxiety. Female subjects in all groups manifested higher death anxiety than male subjects. The effect of age was not significant.

Pratt, Clara Collette., et al., (1985)[6] conducted a study on "Death anxiety and comfort in teaching about death among preschool teachers". This study examined 96 women early childhood educators' death anxiety and their comfort in discussing death with preschool children. Ninety percent believed it was important to be able to discuss death with young children, but only 32 percent felt prepared to do so. Liachers' death anxiety scores were significantly correlated with comfort with dealing with death in the classroom $(R = .30)$. Death anxiety was significantly related to teachers' training in children's understanding of death. No other academic or personal experience factors were significantly related to death anxiety or comfort. However, there was an overall pattern for anxiety and comfort scores to be higher for subjects with the greatest academic and personal experiences in death and dying. Suggestions for teacher education and future investigations are presented.

Thorson, J. A., and Powell, F. C., (1988)[7] conducted a study on "Elements of death anxiety and meanings of death". The objectives of this study were: (1) to test hypotheses that women would have higher death anxiety than men and those older persons would have lower death anxiety than younger people; and (2) to probe for meanings of death among a large, heterogeneous sample. A group of 599 adolescents and adults completed a death anxiety scale; factor analysis of the resultant data revealed seven orthogonal factors. Both hypotheses were supported at acceptable levels of significance. Item analysis revealed additional information on meanings of death: Older respondents indicated a concern over the existence of an afterlife and over loss of personal control; women expressed more fear of pain and bodily decomposition. The strongest finding was variation in death anxiety by age, which confirms Butler's contention that the life review helps the aged to resolve conflicts and relieve anxiety.

Schumaker, J. F., et al., (1991)[8] studied "Death anxiety in Japan and Australia". This study compared death anxiety ratings as measured by the Templer Death Anxiety Scale (Templer, 1970) in 121 Japanese and 139 Australian subjects. Japanese subjects had significantly higher death anxiety scores than their Australian counterparts. Australian women scored significantly higher than Australian men, but no sex differences were found in the Japanese sample. A slight but statistically significant positive correlation was found between age and death anxiety scores. This study contradicted other research that indicated that Eastern cultural attitudes mitigated anxiety about death. These findings are discussed in relation to the complex relationship between culture and death anxiety as well as in relation to problems inherent in our current conception of death anxiety.

D'Attilio, J. P., and Campbell, B., (1991)[9] studied "Relationship between death anxiety and suicide potential in an adolescent population". The relationship between death anxiety and suicide potential was examined in a sample of 62 male and female adolescents whose ages ranged from 16 to 20 yr. A Pearson product-moment correlation between scores on Templer's Death Anxiety Scale and Cull and Gill's Suicide Probability Scale was significant for death anxiety and suicide potential, with higher death anxiety associated with greater suicidal risk. The implications of this association with respect to adolescent suicidal behaviors are discussed.

Rasmussen, C. A., and Brems, C., (1996)[10] conducted a study on "The relationship of death anxiety with age and psychosocial maturity". For this study, 194 respondents completed a biographical data sheet, the Templer (1970) Death Anxiety Scale and the Constantinople (1973) Inventory of Psychosocial Development to help assess the relationship among death anxiety, age, and psychosocial maturity. Findings showed that psychosocial maturity was a better predictor of death anxiety than age was. However, both variables were significantly negatively correlated with death anxiety, revealing that as psychosocial maturity and age increase, death anxiety decreases.

Thorson, J. A., et al., (1999)[11] studied "Age differences in death anxiety among African-American women". Samples of 83 younger and 52 older African-American women completed a death anxiety scale; the younger women had significantly higher scores on the total scale, principally on items dealing with pain, loss of bodily integrity, and decomposition.

Abdel-Khalek, Ahmed M., (2000)[12] studied "Death, Anxiety, And Depression: A Comparison between Egyptian, Kuwaiti, and Lebanese Undergraduates". Three samples of male and female undergraduates were recruited from Egypt (N = 208), Kuwait (N = 215), and Lebanon (N = 228). The Death Anxiety Scale, Death Depression Scale, Trait Anxiety Scale of the State-Trait Anxiety Inventory, and the Beck Depression Inventory were administered to participants in small group sessions in each country. Alpha reliabilities of the four scales in the three nations ranged from almost satisfactory to high levels. In death anxiety, Lebanese subjects had significantly the lowest mean score. As for death depression in males,

Kuwaitis attained the highest mean score, while the Lebanese had the lowest. In females, Egyptians and Kuwaitis had the highest mean death depression scores, while the Lebanese attained the lowest. Regarding the trait anxiety, female Egyptians had the highest mean score, while the Lebanese attained the lowest. The differences between the mean scores of the three nations in the Beck Depression Inventory were not statistically significant. By and large, the gender differences were significant denoting the higher mean scores of females than their male counterparts.

Abdel-Khalek, Ahmed M., (2000-2001)[13] studied "Death, Anxiety, and Depression in Kuwaiti Undergraduates". The present investigation is a replication study on a Kuwaiti sample using the same psychometric instruments which have been previously administered to Egyptian and Lebanese college students. A Kuwaiti sample of undergraduates (N =215) responded to the death anxiety scale (DAS), death depression scale (DDS), as well as the general anxiety (Trait; STAI-T) and general depression (BDI) scales. Administration of the scales was carried out in 1997 98. Alpha reliabilities were high. All of the inter-correlations (r) between the four scales were statistically significant: DAS and DDS r .733, DAS and STAI-T r .412, DAS and BDI r .363, DDS and STAI-T .293, DDS and BDI r .273, and BDI and STAI-T r .739. All the correlations between the last mentioned four scales and gender were statistically significant, that is females attained high scores. Two orthogonal factors were extracted: general neurotic disorder and death distress. The main findings are congruent with previous results on US, Egyptian, and Lebanese participants.

Suhail, K., (2001)[14] studied "Death anxiety in a Pakistani sample". The present study was conducted to find out the incidence s well as the frequency of death anxiety in a Pakistani Muslim sample using the Templer Death Anxiety Scale and Collette-Lester Fear of Death Scale. The interrelationship of death anxiety with the following variables was also investigated: religiosity, anxiety, general well-being and physical health. The findings showed higher death anxiety in Pakistani people compared to other populations. The majority of the subjects reported to fear the uncertainty associated with death the most and they thought about death frequently (almost daily). People lows in general well-being were more anxious of their impending death, whereas those with higher general anxiety were more concerned about death. Religion was not significantly correlated with death anxiety. The results were interpreted in relation to cultural and religious environment specific to Pakistan.

Suhail, Kausar., and Akram, Saima., (2002)[15] in "Correlates of death anxiety in Pakistan" attempted to ascertain the effect of gender, age, and religiosity on death anxiety, 132 participants were interviewed using Templer Death Anxiety Scale and Collette-Lester Fear of Death Scale (CLS). Women, older participants, and less religious participants were found to be more scared of their impending death.

Gender effect was more pronounced, however, on the CLS. Women and less religious people reported to experience greater anxiety than their respective counterparts about different dimensions of death, for example, the shortness of life, total isolation of death, fear of not being, and disintegration of body after dying. The findings of the current work indicate that the general predictors of death anxiety, gender, age, and religiosity reported in Western, predominantly Christian samples also hold in an Eastern, Muslim sample.

In 2003, **Depaola, Stephen J., et al.,**[16] in the article "Death anxiety and attitudes toward the elderly among older adults: the role of gender and ethnicity" investigated the relationship between death anxiety, attitudes toward older adults, and personal anxiety toward one's own aging in a group of 197 older men and women. As predicted, negative attitudes toward other older adults were predicted by personal anxieties about aging and death, and, more specifically, fear of the unknown. In addition, several distinctive anxieties were noted for particular subgroups of respondents. Older women scored higher on the Fear of the Dead subscale of the Multidimensional Fear of Death Scale (MFODS) than did men. Caucasian participants displayed higher Fear of the Dying Process than did older African American participants.

Lastly, older African American participants reported higher levels of death anxiety on 3 of the subscales of the Multidimensional Fear of Death Scale (Fear of the Unknown, Fear of Conscious Death, and Fear for the Body after Death) when compared with older Caucasian participants and also tended to accord less social value to the elderly. These findings are interpreted in terms of patterns of socialization, and their implications for end-of-life care preferences are noted.

Abdel-Khalek, Ahmed M., (2003)[17] studied "Death anxiety in Spain and five Arab countries". The present study compared death anxiety among volunteer undergraduates from Spain and five Arab countries, i.e., Egypt, Kuwait, Qatar, Lebanon, and Syria. The Templer Death Anxiety Scale was used in its Spanish and Arabic forms, respectively. The Mean for the Spanish sample was lower than that of their Arabic counterparts in the five countries, whether the subjects were men or women.

Braunstein, Jeffrey W., (2004)[18] conducted "An Investigation of Irrational Beliefs and Death Anxiety as a Function of HIV Status". The present study investigated the relationship of irrational beliefs and death anxiety as a function of human immunodeficiency virus (HIV) status in homosexual and bisexual men. Recruited for this study were 101 HIV-seropositive participants (34 asymptomatic, 30 symptomatic, and 37 symptomatic and diagnosed with AIDS) and a contrast group (40 HIV-seronegative). In the primary analysis, HIV-negative participants in this study could not be differentiated from asymptomatic, symptomatic, and AIDS diagnosed HIV-infected participants on measures of death anxiety and irrational beliefs regardless of the status or severity of illness. In addition, irrational beliefs strongly predicted death anxiety for all participants. Results from post hoc analyses suggested that HIV status produced an interaction effect with level of total irrational beliefs and together predicted death anxiety. Even in these analyses, total irrational beliefs explained more of the variance of death anxiety than HIV status. These results are discussed within the context of the need for expanding cognitive-behavioral treatment options for HIV-infected individuals.

Abdel-Khalek, Ahmed M., (2004)[19] conducted a study on "Does war affect Death Anxiety Level? Seven Readings of Measurement (1988-2002) before and after the Iraqi invasion of Kuwait". The present study compared death anxiety level in 1988 (i.e., before the Iraqi invasion of Kuwait in 1990) and six readings in the years 1993, 1995, 1996, 1997, 2000, and 2002 (i.e., after the liberation of Kuwait in 1991). The total samples for comparison were 2,221 male and female Kuwaiti volunteer undergraduates. The Arabic version of the Templer Death Anxiety Scale (DAS) was used with all groups. It was found that all the sex-related differences in the same year of the seven testing occasions were significant. For males, the mean DAS scores after the invasion in 1993, 1995, and 1996 were only significantly higher than that before the invasion. With females, there were a number of fluctuations; however, there was a significant increase of the DAS mean score directly after the invasion in comparison with that before it. By and large, the present findings support the Templer's theory regarding death anxiety as a fluid entity influenced by environmental events, particularly war-related experiences.

Campbell, David., and Felts, W Michael., (2005)[20] studied "Effect of the September 11, 2001 terrorist attacks on death anxiety in university students". A sample of 440 undergraduate university students completed the Templer Death Anxiety Scale 2 wk. prior to and 2 wk. after the September 11, 2001 terrorist attacks. Women comprised 66% of the sample, and 79% of the sample identified themselves as 18 to 21 years of age and either freshmen or sophomores. There was no significant mean difference in the pre- and post-terrorist attack Death Anxiety scores. Differences were found on two individual scale items.

Chan, T. H., et al., (2006-2007)[21] conducted a study on "Death preparation and anxiety: a survey in Hong Kong". This study reports the results of a survey on death preparation, death-related beliefs, and death anxiety in a Hong Kong sample. Respondents (N = 285) recruited from the community were asked if they have prepared for themselves a life insurance, a will, and a resting place (e.g. burial site, columbarium, etc.). Questions about their death-related cultural beliefs and anxiety were also asked. Results indicated that respondents who have thought of preparing for their own deaths but not yet acted out (contemplators) held stronger traditional cultural beliefs about death than respondents who have either done the preparations (planners) or never thought of the idea (non-contemplators). Contemplators also reported higher death anxiety. Despite limitations of the study's design, the current results suggest the beliefs in cultural taboo may play a role in the preparation for one's death.

Ens, Carla., and Bond, John B., (2007)[22] in "Death anxiety in adolescents: the contributions of bereavement and religiosity", studied possible relationships between bereavement and religiosity to death anxiety levels of adolescents were investigated. Scales measuring religiosity, bereavement, and death anxiety were incorporated into one questionnaire. Two hundred and twenty-six adolescents between the ages of 11 and 18 participated in the study based in urban and rural private schools within Manitoba. Females exhibited significantly higher death anxiety levels than did males; differences between the death anxiety levels of adolescents having a no-previous-death-experience death and those who had experienced a familial death were not significant; while religiosity levels were significantly higher for students attending religion-based schools, the relationships between measurements of religiosity and death anxiety were weak. Grief due to bereavement was the major factor in determining death anxiety for the adolescent.

Pierce (Jr.), John D., et al., (2007)[23] studied "Gender differences in death anxiety and religious orientation among US high school and college students". Women report both a higher death anxiety and extrinsic religiosity than men, but it is unknown why. Research has not previously linked these findings. We provide two alternative theoretical models of causal links: (a) women's higher death anxiety promotes extrinsic religiosity or (b) women's higher extrinsic religiosity promotes greater death anxiety. High school and college students in the United States (118 young men and 257 young women) completed Templer's (1970) Death Anxiety Scale and the intrinsic and extrinsic religiosity subscales of Allport and Ross (1967) Religious Orientation Scale. Women reported significantly higher levels of death anxiety and extrinsic religiosity. Gender differences in extrinsic religiosity were partially explainable by gender differences in death anxiety. Also, gender differences in death anxiety could partially be explained by gender differences in extrinsic religiosity. This provides future research with some direction in the link between gender, religious orientation, and death anxiety. It also underscores recent arguments that religious motivations vary between cultures and groups.

Mohan Raju, P., (2009)[24] studied "Death anxiety among Ethiopian undergraduate students". Measurement of Death Anxiety among 151 Ethiopian undergraduate students using Templer's scale and Thorson and Powell's scale revealed that the sample has slightly higher than average death anxiety. The results also indicate that in this largely Orthodox Christian sample, students were afraid of the pain in death and less afraid of what happens to their body after death. As some items in each scale did not work well, the Cronbach alphas were low, .61 for the 12 items of Templer's scale and .78 for the 15 items of Thorson and Powell's scale. The correlation between the two full-scale scores was .58 and between scale scores with only acceptable items was .67, indicating the possibility that both scales measure death anxiety equally well if some items are excluded. Results were not consistent with some previous studies in other cultures. Age was significantly related to both Templer's scale (0.29) and Thorson and Powell's scale (0.28). Death anxiety dimensions like time, control, and afterlife aspects seemed to have doubtful meanings in the Ethiopian sample.

2.3 STUDIES IN INDIA

Parsuram, A. and Gandhi, P. (1994)[25] conducted a study on "Beliefs and death anxiety". In the present investigation an attempt has been made to study the importance of certain religious and nonreligious beliefs in managing death anxiety. We believe that human beings adopt beliefs which create a cushioning or comforting effect on the human mind with regard to questions of death and dying. Four such beliefs are 1.Belief in God, 2.Belief in life-after-death, 3.Justice beliefs and 4.Perceived Control beliefs. A total of 90 subjects were selected from three different religious groups viz. Islamic, Christian (RC), and Hindus. A significant difference in the death anxiety scores was expected, with Hindus expected to score lower than the Muslims and Christians. The three groups scored significantly differently on death anxiety. Results on death anxiety support the hypothesis partially as the mean death anxiety score for the Muslims, Christians and Hindus is 5.13, 8.56 and 5.53 respectively. Results related to the chosen beliefs also yielded significantly different mean scores across three religions, and have been discussed within the framework of the functional relevance of these beliefs in managing death-anxiety.

Thingujam, Nutankumar S., & Ram, Usha., (2002)[26] conducted a study on "Death Anxiety among People of Peaceful and Disturbed Areas: A Comparative Study". Thakur and Thakur's Death Anxiety Scale was administered to 365 students (177 from Imphal and 188 from Pune). Results indicated that students from Imphal scored higher on death anxiety than those of Pune. Females also scored higher on death anxiety than males in both the cities. The results have been discussed from the cultural points of view and existing literature.

Madnawat, A. V. Singh., and Kachhawa, P. Singh., (2007)[27] studied "Age, gender, and living circumstances: discriminating older adults on death anxiety". The present study examines the effect of age, gender, and living circumstances on elderly persons' death anxiety. For this purpose, 299 persons attending public parks (avg. age = 70 years) were interviewed using the Death Anxiety Survey Schedule, which is a set of 10 questions related to death anxiety from an Indian perspective. Women, those relatively older, and those living with family were significantly more anxious about the word death. The gender and age results in this Indian sample are similar to that in some western samples. The results that those living with family have significantly higher death anxiety are not in agreement with past western studies and may reflect cultural differences in anxiety about death.

Chengti, S., and Patil, S., (2008)[28] studied "Death anxiety in Senior Citizens". The principal aim of the study has been to assess death anxiety in the elderly. It is assumed that death anxiety is a characteristic and found along the age range commencing from fifties. The theories of aging have proved beyond doubt that death anxiety vibrates in the middle age period. However there is other factors like socio-economic status, educational level, nature of occupation, etc. which are believed to exert their influence on arousal of anxiety in the individuals. Thus the study addresses itself to delineate the factors affecting the level of anxiety of senior citizens residing in Gulbarga. The sample consists of 100 individuals selected from old age institutions and family dwellers. Attempt were made to collect the information like- the level of education, income, religious affiliation, marital status, residing with spouse, etc. which are believed to be related to the amount of anxiety experienced by elderly persons. For the collection of data Death Anxiety Scale (Upinder Dhar, et al., 1998) was administered and the results were subjected to statistical analysis life t-test. Results clearly revealed: (1) educated senior citizens have higher death anxiety, (2) those staying with family members have higher death anxiety than those residing in old-age home, (3) there is a significant difference in the death anxiety between the two age groups, and (4) though there are sex differences in death anxiety, they are not significant.

Suresh Singh (2013)[29] studied "Death anxiety among aged Manipuris, India". This study aims to test hypotheses that people living in the 'Disturbed Area – more dangerous situations' would have higher death anxiety than that of those inhabiting in the 'Non-Disturbed Area – less dangerous situations', and that women and younger persons would have higher death anxiety than men and older persons respectively. A total of 194 participants with age range from 40 to 96 years (M=56.60 years) completed the Death Anxiety Scale (DAS), standardized in the Indian context, consisting of 10 items. t-test results revealed that persons residing in the more dangerous situations had higher death anxiety than that of those living in the less dangerous situations. Women as compared with men and younger persons as compared with older persons tended to be more death anxious. Limitations of the study and suggestions for future research were also discussed.

Review of previous studies revealed that death anxiety is a function of past and present life experiences and conditions and as age and psychosocial maturity increases, death anxiety decreases. Environmental events, particularly war-related experiences influence death anxiety. Sex, religion, culture and age has also effect on death anxiety.

REFERENCE

[1] J. E. Koocher; D. Foster; and J. L. Gogan. (1976). Death Anxiety in normal children and adolescents. *Psychiatria Clinica*, 9(3-4):220-229.
[2] L. A. Tate. (1982). Life Satisfaction and Death Anxiety in Aged Women. *International Journal of Aging & Human Development*, 15(4): 299-306.

[3] P. W. Lee; F. Lieh-Mak; B. K. Hung; and S. L. Luk. (1983-1984). Death Anxiety in Leukemic Chinese Children. *International Journal of Psychiatry Medicine*, 13(4): 281-289.

[4] R. A. Niemeyer; and G. J. Niemeyer. (1984). Death Anxiety and counseling skill in the suicide interventionist. *Suicide & life-threatening behavior*, 14(2):126-131.

[5] M. Mahabeer; and K. Bhana. (1984). The relationship between religion, religiosity and death anxiety among Indian adolescents. *South African Journal of Psychology*, 14:7-9.

[6] Clara Collette Pratt; Jan Hare; and Cheryl Wright. (1985). Death Anxiety and Comfort in teaching about death among preschool teachers. *Death Studies*, 9(5&6):417-425.

[7] J. A. Thorson; and F. C. Powell. (1988). Elements of Death Anxiety and Meanings of Death. *Journal of Clinical Psychology*, 44(5):691-701.

[8] J. F. Schumaker; W. G. Warren; and G. Groth-Marnat. (1991). Death Anxiety in Japan and Australia. *The Journal of Social Psychology*, 131(4): 511-518.

[9] J. P. D'Attilio; and B. Campbell. (1991). Relationship between Death Anxiety and Suicide Potential in an Adolescent Population. *Psychological Reports*, 67(3 Pt. 1): 975-978.

[10] C. A. Rasmussen; and C. Brems. (1996). The relationship of Death Anxiety with age and psychological maturity. *The Journal of Psychology*, 130(2): 141-144.

[11] J. A. Thorson; F. C. Powell; and V. T. Samuel. (1999). Age differences in death anxiety among African-American women. *Psychological reports*, 83(3 Pt. 2): 1173-1174.

[12] Ahmed M. Abdel-Khalek. (2000). Death, Anxiety, and Depression: A Comparison between Egyptian, Kuwaiti, and Lebanese Undergraduates. *OMEGA-Journal of Death and Dying*, 45(3):277-287.

[13] Ahmed M. Abdel-Khalek. (2000-2001). Death, Anxiety, and Depression in Kuwaiti Undergraduates. *OMEGA-Journal of Death and Dying*, 42(4): 309-320.

[14] K. Suhail. (2001). Death Anxiety in a Pakistani sample. *Journal of the Indian Academy of Applied Psychology*, 27(1-2): 19-27.

[15] Kausar Suhail; and Saima Akram. (2002). Correlates of Death Anxiety in Pakistan. *Death Studies*, 26(1): 39-50.

[16] Stephen J. Depaola; Melody Griffin; Jennie R. Young; and Robert A. Niemeyer. (2003). Death anxiety and attitude toward the elderly among older adults: the role of gender and ethnicity. *Death Studies*, 27(4): 335-354.

[17] Ahmed M. Abdel-Khalek. (2003). Death Anxiety in Spain and Five Arab Countries. *Psychological reports*, 93(2): 527-528.

[18] Jeffrey W. Braunstein. (2004). An Investigation of Irrational Beliefs and Death Anxiety as a Function of HIV Status. *Journal of Rational-Emotive & Cognitive-Behavior Therapy*, 22(1): 21-38.

[19] Ahmed M. Abdel-Khalek. (2004). Does War Affect Death Anxiety Level? Seven Readings of Measurements (1998-2002) Before and After the Iraqi Invasion of Kuwait. *Omega- Journal of Death and Dying*, 49(4): 287-297.

[20] David Campbell; and W. Michael Felts. (2005). Effect of the September 11, 2001 terrorist attacks on death anxiety in University students. *Psychological reports*, 95(3 Pt 1):1055-1058.

[21] T. H. Chan; F. M. Chan; A. F. Tin; A. Y. Chow; and C. L. Chan. (2006-2007). Death preparation and anxiety: A Survey of Hong Kong. *Omega (Westport)*, 54(1): 67-78.

[22] Carla Ens; and John B. Bond. (2007). Death anxiety in Adolescents: the contributions of bereavement and religiosity. *Omega*, 55(3): 169-184.

[23] John D. Pierce Jr.; Adam B. Cohen; Jacqueline A. Chambers; and Rachel M. Meade. (2007). Gender Differences in death anxiety and religious orientation among US high school and college students. *Mental Health, Religion & Culture*, 10(2): 143-150.

[24] P. Mohan Raju. (2009). Death anxiety among Ethiopian undergraduate students.

[25] A. Parsuram; and P. Gandhi. (1994). Beliefs and Death Anxiety. *Journal of the Indian Academy of Applied Psychology*, 20(2): 145-152.

[26] Thingujam Nutankumar S.; and Usha Ram. (2002). Death Anxiety among People of Peaceful and Disturbed Areas: A Comparative Study. *Paper presented at the National Conference on Yoga and Indian Approaches to Psychology. Pondicherry. India. September 29-October 1, 2002.* Unpublished document.

[27] A. V. Singh Madnawat; and P. Singh Kachhawa. (2007). Age, Gender, and Living Circumstances: Discriminating Older Adults on Death Anxiety. *Death Studies*, 31: 763-769.

[28] S. Chengti; and S. Patil. (2008). Death Anxiety in senior Citizens. *Asian Journal of Psychology and Education*, 41(1-2): 9-16.

[29] Rajkumar Suresh Singh. (2013). Death Anxiety among Aged Manipuris, India. *ZENITH International Journal of Multidisciplinary Research*, 3(1): 209-216.

CHAPTER – 3
METHOD AND PROCEDURE

Anything to be done properly must be planned before hand. This part helps the researcher to proceed directly without confusion with the concomitant events. This part of proposal outlines the entire research plans. It describes just what must be done, how it will done, what data will be needed, which data gathering device will be employed, how sources of data will be selected and how the data will be analyzed and conclusion reached. Taking into consideration the above facts, it is essential for the investigator to explain the procedure and techniques, tools, methods of adopting samples, administration of tools, collection of data and organization of data.

As stated earlier, the main objective of the study is to ascertain the death anxiety among post-graduate students of Manipur University. In order to attain the objective, the study was designed using the pattern of normative survey method. Therefore, in this survey research method, questionnaire technique was considered as on-usual device for collecting data for the purpose of evaluation. With the questionnaire method, it was possible to study the death anxiety of a large population in a limited time.

2.1 METHOD OF STUDY

There are various ways and means of collecting, analyzing and reporting research data depending on the problem. There are mainly three types of methods of research:-
(i)   Historical Method;
(ii)   Experimental Method and
(iii)   Descriptive or Normative Method.

Historical approach to the study of any subject denotes an effort to recount some aspect of past life. The possible field of historical research is as broad as life itself. The Experimental method is educational research which is the application and adoption of the classical method of scientific laboratory. Though it is the most difficult of all method, yet it is very important method.

Descriptive methods are designed to obtain pertinent and precise information concerning the current status of phenomenon and whenever possible, to draw valid general conclusions from the facts discovered. They are restricted not only to fact findings but may often results in the formation of important principles of knowledge and solution of significant problems concerning local, state and national and international issues. It studies and investigates phenomena in their natural setting, their purpose of both immediate and long range.

Descriptive method helps to explain educational phenomena in terms of the conditions or relationship that exist, opinion that are hold by the students, teachers, parents and experts, processes that are going on, effect that are evident, or trends that are developing. It is a means through which opinions, attitudes, suggestions for improvement of educational practices and instruction, and other data can be obtained. It is more than just a collection of data; they involved measurement, classification, analysis, comparison and interpretation.

The survey method to educational problem is one of the most commonly used approach and it is one of the important category of descriptive or normative survey method. It is followed in studying local as well as national and international aspects of education. It goes much more beyond gathering and tabulation of data. It involves interpretation, comparison, measurement, classification, evolution and generalization of educational problems. This study is based on survey method, particularly the normative survey research. In view of the purpose of the study, only the survey method has been considered most appropriate.

The case study method is a very popular form of qualitative analysis and involves a careful and complete observation of a social unit, be it a person, a family, an institution, a cultural group or even the entire community. It is a method of study in depth rather than breath. The case study places more emphasis on the full analysis of a limited number of events or conditions and their interrelationship. Thus, case study is essentially an intensive investigation of a particular unit under consideration. The object of the case study is to locate the factors that account for the behavior-patterns of the given unit as an integrated totality. Thus, for the present study, case study method employing methods of descriptive survey research is adopted taking into account the objectives of the study.

2.2 SAMPLES

The sample has been defined as "a miniature picture of the entire group of aggregate from which data was selected. In other words, it is the representative proportion of the population."

For the present study, the investigator selected 391 (three hundred and ninety-one) postgraduate students of Manipur University on the basis of random sampling technique. The demographics of the sample are given in

Table-1:

TABLE 1: SAMPLE OF THE STUDY

MALE	FEMALE	TOTAL
192	199	391

2.3 TOOLS USED

For collecting new unknown data required for the study of any problem, one may use various devices. For each and every type of research, it needs certain instruments together with new facts to explore new fields. The instruments thus employed are called tool. Tools are means for collection of data for interpretation and to explore new fields. The selection of a tool is a difficult task in research and is dependent up on various considerations such as objective of the study, hypotheses of the study, availability of time, availability of the tool itself, personal competence of the investigator to administer the tests and the likes.

For this problem entitled "Death Anxiety among students: A Case-study of Manipur University", the major tool used was questionnaire, which was used for measuring the death anxiety of post-graduate students of Manipur University as it was thought to be more flexible tool for collecting both qualitative and quantitative information. **Death Anxiety Scale (DAS)**[1] standardized by Upinder Dhar, Savita Mehta and Santosh Dhar (1998) consisting of 10 (ten) items of Yes/No alternatives measuring the degree of death anxiety by various surroundings and diseases was used for collection of primary data. Related and relevant literatures were reviewed as secondary sources of data.

3.3(A) DEVELOPMENT OF THE DEATH ANXIETY SCALE

After consulting relevant literatures, numbers of items were developed. Each item was transferred on a card. A panel of 50 judges was prepared. Definition of death anxiety was written on card along with necessary instructions for selection of the cards. The cards were placed before each judge who was contacted individually. The choice for categorization of each card/item was noted and the frequency of choice was calculated. The items which were chosen 75 percent or more were spotted out. Since the scale was not designed to measure proficiency, difficulty index was not considered. The final form of the scale constituted 10 (ten) items *(Appendix A)*.

3.3(B) VALIDITY

Besides face validity, as all items of the scale are concerned with the variable under focus, the scale has high content validity. It is evident from the assessment and rating of the judges/experts that items of the scale are directly related to the concept of death anxiety. In order to determine validity from the coefficient of reliability (Garrett, 1981), the reliability index was calculated. The later has indicated high validity on account of being 0.93.

3.3(C) RELIABILITY

The reliability of the scale was determined by calculating split-half reliability coefficient, corrected for full length, on a sample of 200 subjects (25-55 years). The split-half reliability coefficient was= 0.87.

3.3(D) NORMS

Norms for the scale are available on a sample of subjects belonging to the age-range of 25-55 years. These norms should be regarded as reference points for interpreting the Death Anxiety scores. However, norms are based on the sample drawn from Rohtak and Delhi. The users of the scale would be well advised to develop their own norms based on their own samples.

An individual with a very high score i.e., above $(M+1\sigma)$, may be considered to have very high level of death anxiety, symptomatic of such high state that is likely to have a disruptive and interfering influence on his performance, especially on complex activities and individual concerned may be in need of counseling or psychotherapy. The low score i.e., above $(M-1\sigma)$, would indicate people who have very low level of death anxiety. The scores lying within $(M\pm1\sigma)$ would represent especially "normal" individuals with moderately good drive to stimulate performance without any interference of any kind of anxiety under focus.

TABLE 2: NORMS FOR INTERPRETATION OF THE RAW SCORES

Mean (M)	=	5.42
Standard Deviation (σ) =		1.62
Normal Range $(M\pm1\sigma)$=		3.80-7.04
High	=	7.05 and above
Low	=	3.79 and below

3.3(E) USE OF THE SCALE

Like other psychometric tests of this nature, its primary and proper utility lies with work on large groups, whether for research, survey process, or for comparison of populations. The scale can be successfully used for screening out individuals who suffer from alarmingly high degree of death anxiety which has a disruptive, inhibiting or interfering influence on the day-to-day life and performance. The scale is likely to be a useful tool in the armory of a psychologist. It gives a measure of death anxiety for experimental, clinical and counseling purposes when subject can spare only half an hour or so. It is self-administering and does not require the services of a highly trained tester. It is eminently suitable for group administration as well as for individual testing.

3.3(F) INSTRUCTIONS FOR ADMINISTRATION AND SCORING

1.   The instructions printed on the response sheet are sufficient to take care of the questions that are asked.
2.   No time limit should be given for completing the scale. However, most of the respondents should finish it in about seven to eight minutes, though there may always be a few individuals who would take much longer time.
3.   Before administering the scale, it is advisable to emphasize orally that responses should be checked as quickly as possible and sincere cooperation is required for the same. The respondents should be told that the results of the scale would help in self-knowledge and that responses would always remain strictly confidential.
4.   It should also be emphasized that there is no right or wrong answer to the statements. The statements are designed to have differences in individual's reactions to various situations. The scale is meant to know the difference between individuals and is not meant to rank them as good or bad, right or wrong, desirable or undesirable.

5. It should be duly emphasized that all the statements have to be responded in either positive or negative and no statement is to be left unanswered.

6. It is not desirable to tell the subjects the exact purpose for which the test is used. If the subject is of "inquisitive type" assesses the reactions of individuals in varying vague answers like "the test measures personality", "it situations", etc. should be given.

7. Though the scale is self-administering, it has been found useful to read out the instructions printed on the response sheet to the subjects.

8. Manual scoring is done conveniently. No scoring key or stencil is provided.

9. Each item or statement which is checked as "Yes" or "No" should be awarded the score of "1' or "0" respectively. The sum of scores of all the ten items is the DA-Score.

3.4 STATISTICAL TECHNIQUE USED [2]

In order to analyze and interpret the test scores, the investigator adopted the following statistical procedure-

(i) Mean,
(ii) Standard deviation and
(iii) t-test to compare same sub-group.

REFERENCES

[1] Upinder Dhar, Savita Mehta and Santosh Dhar. (1998). Manual for Death Anxiety Scale. Agra, India: National Psychological Corporation.

[2] Henry E. Garrett (2007). Statistics in Psychology and Education, 12th reprint. Delhi: Paragon International Publishers.

CHAPTER – 4

ANALYSIS AND INTERPRETATION OF DATA

In the preceding chapters, the background of the study, review of related literature and the method and procedure have been provided. The next step was to analyze and interpret the data in the light of the objectives of the study. As stated in Chapter 1, the main purpose of the present study is to study the death anxiety among post-graduate students of Manipur University with special reference to the sex.

In the present study, the measure of the central tendency (Arithmetic Mean) and the measure of dispersion (Standard Deviation) were applied to study the nature of the data. t-test was applied to study the significant difference between male and female post-graduate students of Manipur University.

4.1 STATISTICAL COMPUTATIONS

4.1.1 Calculation of Mean

1Mean is a mathematical average and it is the most popular measure of central tendency. The group average for the item was calculated. The investigator followed the short method in computing the mean. The researcher calculated directly from the raw scores. The researcher summed up the measurement and then divided by the number of measurement of cases. In terms of formula:

Mean or m $= \dfrac{\Sigma f x}{N}$

Where,

f= frequency

x= scores

N= Number of samples.

4.1.2 Calculation of Standard Deviation

Further, the investigator also calculated the Standard Deviation of all the groups in the test by using the raw scores method or from the original measurement. This method has been found reasonable as the number of measurement is not long, the obtained values are small numbers and moreover, a calculating machine was available to the investigator.

The standard deviation of a group score is a number which tells us whether most of those scores cluster closely around their mean or are spread out along the scale. The standard deviation is useful not only for describing distributions but also for comparing groups. Furthermore, it provides the basis for standardizing test scores by computing.

The formula for calculation of standard deviation may be represented as:

$$s = \sqrt{s^2}$$

$$\text{where } s^2 = \frac{\Sigma (x-c)^2 - nk^2}{(n-1)}$$

x= a score,
n= the number of scores,
c= the whole part of the mean and
k= the fractional part of the mean.

STEPS FOR CALCULATING STANDARD DEVIATION:

Step1. List all the scores and find their mean.

Step2. Compute the sum of squared deviations.
To do this:
First, subtract from each score the whole-number part (c) of the mean. Record the result for each score in a column next to the list of scores. These results are the deviations (x-c).
Second, multiply each deviation by itself to get the squared deviations $(x-c)^2$ of each score.
Third, add up all the squared deviations to get their sum $\Sigma (x-c)^2$.

36

Step3. Subtract the quantity nk ^{2} from the result of step2.

The fractional part of the mean, k, is squared and then multiplied by number of scores, n. This product is then subtracted from the result of step2 i.e. $\sum (x-c)$ ^{2} - nk ^{2}

Step4. Compute the variance, s^2.

This is accomplished by dividing the result of step3 by a number that is one less than the number of scores (n-1).

i.e. $s^2 = \sum (x-c)$ ^{2} – nk^2 / (n-1).

Step5. Compute the standard deviation, s.

To get the standard deviation, take the square root of the value obtained at the end of step 4, i.e. s=√s^2

Step6. Interpret the statistics.

The larger the standard deviation, the more spread out the scores. A small standard deviation will be found when the scores all cluster to the mean.

4.1.3 Calculation of t-test:

To judge the significance of difference between the means of the variable, investigator also calculated the t-test. This method is found reasonable as the population variance is not known and assumed to be equal.

The t-test is a test to see if there is a statistically significant difference between the mean scores of two groups. The t-test is a quick way of accomplishing the same end. It answers the question: Is the obtained difference between the means bigger than the differences expected to obtain if the two groups were actually equivalent? In other words, is the obtained difference bigger than the expected difference which could have occurred by chance sampling variations? If the obtained t-value is larger than the tabled t-value, this means that the obtained difference between means is larger than would be expected if the groups were not really different.

STEPS FOR CALCULATION OF T-TEST:

Step1. Prepare input data.

For each group, compute the mean score, m, and the standard deviation, s, and record these values in the Descriptive Statistics Table as shown below along with the number, n, of scores of each group.

TABLE 3: DESCRIPTIVE STATISTICS TABLE

GROUP	NUMBER OF SCORES, (n)	MEAN OF SCORES, (m)	STANDARD DEVIATION, (s)
Group A	N_a	M_a	S_a
Group B	N_b	M_b	S_b

Step2. Compute (M_a-M_b), the difference between group means.

Step3. Compute S_d

Multiply S_a by itself. Then multiply the result by $(N_a -1)$ i.e. one less than the number of scores in the Group A.

$$(S_a)^2(N_a-1)$$

a. Multiply S_b by itself. Then multiply the result by $(N_b -1)$ i.e. one less than the number of scores in the Group B.

$$(S_b)^2(N_b-1)$$

b. Add the result of Substep a. and Substep b.

$$(S_a)^2(N_a-1)+ (S_b)^2(N_b-1)$$

c. Add N_a and N_b and subtract 2 from the same.

$$(N_a + N_b)-2$$

e. Divide the result of Substep c by the result of Substep d

$$\{(S_a)^2(N_a-1)+ (S_b)^2(N_b-1)\}/ (N_a + N_b)-2$$

f. Divide 1 by number of scores of Group A.

$$1/ N_a$$

g. Divide 1 by number of scores of Group B.

$$1/ N_b$$

h. Add the results of Substep f and Substep g.

$$(1/ N_a + 1/ N_b)$$

i. Now multiply the result of Substep e by result of Substep h.

$$\{(S_a)^2(N_a-1)+ (S_b)^2(N_b -1)\}/ (N_a + N_b)-2 \times (1/ nA+1/ nB)$$

j. Find the square root of Substep i. This is S_d.

$$S_d = \sqrt{\{(S_a)^2(N_a-1)+ (S_b)^2(N_b -1)\}/ (N_a + N_b)-2 \times (1/ nA+1/ nB)}$$

Step4. Compute t.

Divide the result of Step2 by the result of Step3, Substep j. This value is the obtained t-value.

$$\textbf{Obtained t-value} = (M_a - M_b)/ S_d$$

Step5. Find the tabled t-value.

Step6. Interpret the statistics.

The obtained t-value may have been negative or positive. Ignore the negative sign if there is one, and compute the absolute size of the obtained t-value with the tabled t-value. If the obtained t-value is larger than the tabled t-value, then the difference between the two groups is statistically significant in the conventional sense. If the obtained t-value is smaller or not larger than the tabled t-value, then the difference between the two groups is not statistically significant, this indicates that the differences could have been the result of chance.

Thus, the working formula for calculation of t-test may be represented as:

$$\textbf{t-value} = (M_a - M_b)/ S_d \text{ where}$$

M_a = mean of Group A;

M_b = mean of Group B and

S_d = a standard deviation.

4.2   DEATH ANXIETY AMONG POST-GRADUATE STUDENTS

Hypothesis1:

The Death Anxiety is high among Post-graduate students.
The Death Anxiety Scores on the Death Anxiety Scale (DAS) among Post-graduate students of Manipur University is given in Table 4.

TABLE 4: Death Anxiety Scores of Post-graduate Students.

Number of Samples (n)	Mean of Scores (m)	Standard Deviation (s)
391	6.93	2.21

From above table, it can be observed that the overall mean on death anxiety was 6.93, which indicates the normal range of death anxiety level among post-graduate students of Manipur University. Thus, the hypothesis is rejected. The Death Anxiety among Post-graduate students of Manipur University was found to be normal. It was expected that the death anxiety would be high among the Post-graduates.

Thus, the hypothesis that the Death Anxiety is high among Post-graduate students fails to be accepted.

Hypothesis2:

There is no significant difference in Death Anxiety between Male and Female students.

The significance of difference in the mean Death Anxiety scores of male and female Post-graduate students of Manipur University is presented in Table5 below:

TABLE 5: Comparison of Mean, Standard Deviation and t-test of Post-graduate students on Death Anxiety.

Sex	Number of Samples (n)	Mean of Scores (m)	Standard Deviation (s)	t-value
Male	192	6.11	2.27	2.3*
Female	199	7.72	1.84	

* p≤0.05. (Stands for significance at 0.05 level).

It can be observed from the Table5 that the Death Anxiety Score of female as compared with male Post-graduate students of Manipur University exhibited higher level of death anxiousness {m=7.72 v/s 6.11 respectively, t(389)=2.3, p≤0.05}. t-test revealed that the differences in Death Anxiety is statistically significant.

Thus, the hypothesis that there is no significant difference in Death Anxiety between male and female Post-graduate students also fails to be accepted. And female students had more death anxiety than male students.

CHAPTER – 4

MAIN FINDINGS, EDUCATIONAL IMPLICATIONS AND SUGGESTIONS FOR FURTHER STUDIES

5.1 MAIN FINDINGS

Current results revealed that the overall death anxiety of the respondents was normal. A significant difference was found between female and male students with female being more death anxious. The result is in consistent with other previous studies (e.g., Mahabeer and Bhana, 1984; Niemeyer, 1986; Abdel-Khalek & Omar, 1988; Dattel & Niemeyer, 1990; Schumaker et al., 1991; Niemeyer & Fortner, 1995; Suhail & Akram, 2002; Nutankumar & Usha Ram, 2002; Madnawat & Kachhawa, 2007, Ens & Bond, 2007; Suresh Singh, 2013).

The present study is limited in populations and variables studied. The generalizability of the results emerged from this study to other populations would seem to merit further study. Despite the limitations of the study's design, we may have an insight into the possible relationship sex and death anxiety. The death anxiety level of the people of different ages and the reasons for higher or lower death anxiety may be explored through further studies on a larger population incorporating other variables.

5.2 EDUCATIONAL IMPLICATIONS

This study was undertaken to ascertain the level of death anxiousness of the post-graduate students of Manipur University. The findings of the study show that the overall mean death anxiety score is normal. Sex difference was, however, observed. Female subjects in the group manifested higher death anxiety than male subjects. Male students were in the normal range whereas the female students were high on the death anxiety scale. Therefore, teachers, policy makers and educational planners should arrange special "anxiety management" programmes meant for the students as well as the teachers.

Education is an instrument of social change and development in a society based on the grounds of strong theory of practical applicability. Subjects such as psychology, anxiety management, sociology besides various other subjects must be given due emphasis in the light of the present findings. Higher degree courses in psychology, sociology and anxiety management must be introduced at the University level so as to have a more scientific study in the area and provide remedial measures.

5.3 SUGGESTIONS FOR FURTHER STUDIES

Some of the suggestions for further studies could be as under:

1. A study of death anxiety of senior citizens.
2. The same study can be conducted among the college students.
3. A comparative study of death anxiety between young and older adults can be conducted.
4. The present study was confined only to Manipur University. Similar study can be conducted on other Universities.
5. A comparative study of death anxiety among the post-graduate students of different states can be studied.

CHAPTER – 6
SUMMARY

6.1 INTRODUCTION

It has been the practice to treat death anxiety as a uniform or single entity, without recognizing the underlying typology. The importance of refining that concept comes from clinical findings that different types of traumatic events lead to different forms of death anxiety, each of which is experienced and responded to by humans in a distinctive manner. These responses are both conscious and unconscious i.e. within or outside direct awareness. The former are generally well known and these include traumatic and post-traumatic stress syndromes and responses to cancer and other types of grave illness. But it is not generally appreciated that death anxiety is prompted by every type of traumatic event and that it can register and operate entirely outside of awareness. The effects, nonetheless, are powerful and often devastating, and always include a tightening of communication defenses in an effect to obliterate the conscious recognition of the various ways that a given trauma is imparting on the individual and the extent to which death-related anxieties have been activated.

6.2 DEATH ANXIETY

Death anxiety refers to the fear and apprehension of one's own death. It is the neurotic fear of loss of the self which in intense state parallels feelings of helplessness and depression. Man's awareness of his own death produces anxiety that can only be dealt with by recognizing one's individuality. Man's awareness of death gives him the responsibility of finding meaning in life.

Death is a biological, personal, socio-cultural and existential phenomenon (Baron, 2001). Knowledge of people's concerns and fears regarding death and dying has important theoretical and practical implications

44

in addressing issues around end-of-life care (Tang et al., 2002). The biological death is useful to distinguish between the process of aging and the ending called death. Yet when the actual time comes, and the individual faces death alone, the psychological reactions appear to be remarkably similar.

Elizabeth Kübler-Ross (1969) found that in the majority of persons, almost regardless of age, the personal reactions to imminent death pass through five phases- Denial, Anger, Bargaining, Depression and Acceptance (although not every individual achieves the final phase). Dying and death, like other major aspects of human life, are also very important cultural and social phenomena.

The death can be fully understood only if it is viewed as one of the central meanings of human existence. An idea of the centrality of one's own death can be gathered if individuals could be made to contemplate seriously the possibility of their own death (McCarthy, 1980).

As death is the final stage of life cycle, it can be approached naturally by dying individuals and their families. Death and dying can be seen as a part of life process, or they can be viewed as a dramatic, painful, tortured experience both for the individual and the families. Increasingly, more research reports are being presented on the nature of death and dying. Research on exactly when death occurs, how the dying should be treated, and how their families might better cope will continue for many years (Lefton, 1982).

Even though death most commonly occurs in later years, it may happen at any stage of life. Accidents and suicides are the major causes of death among younger persons, and continue to be so in later years, although their relative significance declines. Often death is associated with some special psychological stress, it may be acute mourning, or an anniversary, or some particular loss of status or self-esteem.

Death is sometimes defined as the absence of certain clinically detectable vital signs. More recently, death has sometimes been defined as the lack of brain wave activity. Still other says that death can only be defined as a bodily state which represents an irreversible loss of vital functions and from which the individual cannot possibly be retrieved. According to the concept of terminal drop, death can be predicted from certain dramatic changes in cognitive function in the period preceding demise, i.e., significant changes both in personal adjustment and performance may serve as indicators of impeding death (Reigal & Reigal, 1972).

The meaning of life and death vary from one individual to another (Kübler, 1975). The act of dying itself may involve a certain amount of "anticipatory self grief", grief over the loss of one's own life- that, fears what it may be to lose one's self. In addition, fear of dying is often associated with unfounded beliefs that dying itself is quite painful, that one may be abandoned by everyone when dying, that death involves an ultimate aloneness, and "that there may be final medical procedure that will further dehumanize oneself by being turned into a sort of plumbing shop...".(Holocomb, 1975).

The fear of pain can be relieved by the knowledge of modern pain relieving processes. It can help to know that though dying is rarely pleasant, it is neither as painful nor as unpleasant as is often feared. Fear of dying involves not only physiological but psychological factors, too. Pain is more easily dealt with than loneliness.

Robert Langs (1997)   identified three classes of death anxiety-

> 1.*Predatory Death Anxiety:* This form is the oldest phylogenetically in the cellular organisms which have receptors that have evolved to react to external dangers and they also possess self-protective, responsive mechanisms designed to insure survival in the face of chemical and physical forms of attack or danger. In humans, this form of death anxiety is evolved by a variety of dangerous situations that put the recipient at risk or threatens his or her survival. These traumas may be psychological and/or physical. Predatory death anxieties mobilizes an individual's adaptive resource and lead to fight or flight, active efforts to combat the danger or attempts to escape the threatening situation.

These responses also may take mental and/or physical forms, and include both conscious and unconscious processing and modes of adapting.

2. *Predation Death Anxiety:* This form of death anxiety arises when an individual harms others physically and/or mentally. The arousal of this type of anxiety often involves unconscious rather than conscious realizations and processing. The primary reaction to this type of anxiety is that of conscious and unconscious guilt, which, in turn, motivates a variety of self-punitive decisions and actions by the perpetrator of harm to others whose deeper sources go unappreciated.

3. *Existential Death Anxiety:* This is the most powerful form of death anxiety and its activation is based in humans on the definitive, conscious awareness and anticipation of the inevitability of personal demise. This expectation and the anxieties it evokes are the result of human language awareness of the distinction of personal identity, and the ability to anticipate the future. Humans defended against this type of death anxiety through denial, which is effected through a wide range of mental mechanisms and physical actions, which may also go unrecognized. While limited use of denial tends to be adaptive, its use is usually excessive and proves to be costly emotionally.

Although humans have always thought about death, empirical research on death anxiety didn't begin in earnest until the late 1950s (Dulark, 2002). The fear of death has been rated as the most common and the second worst fear that troubles us (Rattan, 2005). Many are traumatized long before they near their end from their impending death. Many suffer from death anxiety but are able to function.

Death anxiety is defined as an abnormally great fear of death, with feelings of dread or apprehension arising when one thinks about the process of dying or what happens after death (Webster's, 1980). Longman Dictionary of Psychology and Psychiatry (1984) defines death anxiety as "a depressive state in which anxiety over dying and fear of death (thanatophobia) are salient symptoms". Death anxiety has been defined as "a point of view of dying, a part of the fabric of being the child develops before a precise conceptual formulation, that is, it exists prior to and outside of language and image" (Ireland, 1993).

6.3   STATEMENT OF THE PRESENT PROBLEM

The study explores the degree of death anxiety among students undergoing post-graduate courses in Manipur University. Further attempt was also made to find out the difference in death anxiety according to sex.

6.4   RATIONALE OF THE STUDY

Since ancient times, human beings have searched for the *"Fountain of Youth"*- some means prolonged youth, and life, indefinitely. But alas, such dreams have remained only illusions; while life and health can be prolonged through proper diet, exercise and reduced exposure to various sources of stress, there appears to be no way to live forever.

Death is the inevitable end of life. Changing environment, conflicts and dreaded diseases has been the one of the causes of death anxiety all over the world. News of murder, bomb-attacks, death, especially 'bullet-deaths', has become a "regular news item" of the local dailies. In a conflict situation prevailing in the state, the environment for education has become polluted.

Manipur, a small State in the North-Eastern India, is better known in the world to-day as a strife-torn place. Though populated only by 22, 93, 896 persons as per the Census of India, 2001, (Statistical Abstract Manipur 2005), Manipur is within 36 areas of conflict zones of the world as identified by Uppsala Conflict Data Programme (UCDP) (2008).

Approximately 30 (thirty) armed groups (non-state actors) were reported to be operating in and around the State (Prakash, 2008). Demands for sovereignty and homeland were the basic objectives of these armed groups. As a result, the entire State has been in turmoil for the last five decades. In order to tackle the armed activities and to assist the civil administration, the whole State was declared as 'Disturbed Area' on September 8, 1980.

In the recent past, Manipur experienced major upheavals or social drama and the educational institutions remained 'closed' for more than four months. Such situations/conditions cater to creation of imbalances in the society. Almost every person in Manipur has   death-related experiences in one way or the other.

Death related trauma may lead to constructive actions, more often than not; they lead to actions that are, in the short or long run, damaging of self or others. The present study attempts to study the death anxiety among post-graduate students. The study is felt significant by the researcher because at the time of stress, and especially when the scepter of death anxiety has been activated, it is important to be on the alert for decisions and actions that are unconsciously motivated by the need to deny death because they almost prove exceedingly costly for all concerned. In such conflict situation education is always at stake.

The findings may be of practical value to the planners and policy makers in providing the necessary feedback to the student community reading in the highest educational institution.

6.5   OBJECTIVES OF THE STUDY

The objectives of the present study were:

(i)   To study the death anxiety among post-graduate students.

(ii)   To find out the difference in death anxiety between male and female students.

(iii)   To suggest remedial measures for improving the existing situation.

6.6 HYPOTHESES OF THE STUDY

(i) The death anxiety is high among University students.

(ii) There is no significant difference in death anxiety between male and female students.

6.7 METHOD OF THE STUDY:

For the present study, case study method employing methods of descriptive survey research is adopted taking into account the objectives of the study.

6.8 SAMPLES

For the present study, the investigator selected 391 (three hundred and ninety-one) postgraduate students of Manipur University on the basis of random sampling technique. The demographics of the sample are given in **Table-6:**

TABLE 6: SAMPLE OF THE STUDY

MALE	FEMALE	TOTAL
192	199	391

6.9 TOOLS USED

For this problem **Death Anxiety Scale (DAS)** [1] standardized by Upinder Dhar, Savita Mehta and Santosh Dhar (1998) consisting of 10 (ten) items of Yes/No alternatives measuring the degree of death anxiety by various surroundings and diseases was used for collection of primary data. The reliability of the scale determined by calculating split-half reliability coefficient was= **0.87** and validity being **0.93**.

6.9(a) NORMS

Norms for the scale are available on a sample of subjects belonging to the age-range of 25-55 years. These norms should be regarded as reference points for interpreting the Death Anxiety scores.

An individual with a very high score i.e., above $(M+1\sigma)$, may be considered to have very high level of death anxiety, symptomatic of such high state that is likely to have a disruptive and interfering influence on his performance, especially on complex activities and individual concerned may be in need of counseling or psychotherapy. The low score i.e., above (M-1 σ), would indicate people who have very low level of death anxiety. The scores lying within (M±1σ) would represent especially "normal" individuals with moderately good drive to stimulate performance without any interference of any kind of anxiety under focus.

TABLE 7: Norms for Interpretation of the Raw Scores

Mean (M)	=	5.42
Standard Deviation (σ) =		1.62
Normal Range (M±1 σ)	=	3.80-7.04
High	=	7.05 and above
Low	=	3.79 and below

6.10 MAIN FINDINGS

Current results revealed that the overall death anxiety of the respondents was normal. A significant difference was found between female and male students with female being more death anxious. The result is in consistent with other previous studies (e.g., Mahabeer and Bhana, 1984; Niemeyer, 1986; Abdel-Khalek & Omar, 1988; Dattel & Niemeyer, 1990; Schumaker et al., 1991; Niemeyer & Fortner, 1995; Suhail & Akram, 2002; Nutankumar & Usha Ram, 2002; Madnawat & Kachhawa, 2007, Ens & Bond, 2007; Suresh Singh, 2013).

The present study is limited in populations and variables studied. The generalizability of the results emerged from this study to other populations would seem to merit further study. Despite the limitations of the study's design, we may have an insight into the possible relationship sex and death anxiety. The death anxiety level of the people of different ages and the reasons for higher or lower death anxiety may be explored through further studies on a larger population incorporating other variables.

6.11 EDUCATIONAL IMPLICATIONS

This study was undertaken to ascertain the level of death anxiousness of the post-graduate students of Manipur University. The findings of the study show that the overall mean death anxiety score is normal. Sex difference was, however, observed. Female subjects in the group manifested higher death anxiety than male subjects. Male students were in the normal range whereas the female students were high on the death anxiety scale. Therefore, teachers, policy makers and educational planners should arrange special "anxiety management" programmes meant for the students as well as the teachers.

Education is an instrument of social change and development in a society based on the grounds of strong theory of practical applicability. Subjects such as psychology, anxiety management, sociology besides various other subjects must be given due emphasis in the light of the present findings. Higher degree courses in psychology, sociology and anxiety management must be introduced at the University level so as to have a more scientific study in the area and provide remedial measures.

6.12 SUGGESTIONS FOR FURTHER STUDIES

Some of the suggestions for further studies could be as under:

1. A study of death anxiety of senior citizens.
2. The same study can be conducted among the college students.
3. A comparative study of death anxiety between young and older adults can be conducted.
4. The present study was confined only to Manipur University. Similar study can be conducted on other Universities.
5. A comparative study of death anxiety among the post-graduate students of different states can be studied.

BIBLIOGRAPHY

Abdel-Khalek, Ahmed M. (2000). Death, Anxiety, and Depression: A Comparison between Egyptian, Kuwaiti, and Lebanese Undergraduates. *OMEGA-Journal of Death and Dying,* 45(3):277-287.

Abdel-Khalek, Ahmed M. (2000-2001). Death, Anxiety, and Depression in Kuwaiti Undergraduates. *OMEGA-Journal of Death and Dying,* 42(4): 309-320.

Abdel-Khalek, Ahmed M. (2003). Death Anxiety in Spain and Five Arab Countries. *Psychological reports,* 93(2): 527-528.

Abdel-Khalek, Ahmed M. (2004). Does War Affect Death Anxiety Level? Seven Readings of Measurements (1998-2002) Before and After the Iraqi Invasion of Kuwait. *Omega- Journal of Death and Dying,* 49(4): 287-297.

Aggarwal, J. C. (1995). Essentials of Educational Psychology. New Delhi: Vikas Publishing House Pvt. Ltd.

Aggarwal, J. C. (2001). Basic Ideas of Educational Psychology. New Delhi: Shipra Publication.

Aggarwal, Dr. Y. P. (1998). The Science of Educational Research: A Source Book. Kurukshetra: Nirmal Book Agency.

Aggarwal, Y. P. (2004). Statistical Methods: Concepts, Application and Computation, 3rd ed., New Delhi: Sterling Publishers Pvt. Ltd.

Baron, Robert A. (2001). Psychology, 3rd ed., New Delhi: Prentice Hall of India Private Limited.

Best, John W. (1977). Research in Education. New Delhi: Prentice Hall of India.

Bischof, L. J. (1976). Adult Psychology. New York: Harper and Row.

Braunstein, Jeffrey W. (2004). An Investigation of Irrational Beliefs and Death Anxiety as a Function of HIV Status. *Journal of Rational-Emotive & Cognitive-Behaviour Therapy,* 22(1): 21-38.

Campbell, David and Felts, W. Michael. (2005). Effect of the September 11, 2001 terrorist attacks on death anxiety in University students. *Psychological reports,* 95(3 Pt 1):1055-1058.

Chandra, Soti Shivendra & Sharma, Rajendra K. (1997). Research in Education. New Delhi: Atlantic Publishers and Distributors.

Chaube, S. P. & Chaube, Akhilesh (1999). Educational Psychology. Agra: Laxmi Narain Agarwal.

Chauhan, S. S. (1983). Advanced Educational Psychology, 5th ed., Ghaziabad: Vikas Publishing House Pvt. Ltd.

Chengti, S. and Patil, S. (2008). Death Anxiety in senior Citizens. *Asian Journal of Psychology and Education,* 41(1-2): 9-16.

Collins Standard Dictionary. (1978). New Delhi: Oxford and IBH Publishing Co.

D'Attilio, J. P. and Campbell, B. (1991). Relationship between Death Anxiety and Suicide Potential in an Adolescent Population. *Psychological Reports,* 67(3 Pt. 1): 975-978.

Depaola, Stephen J.; Griffin, Melody; Young, Jennie R.; and Niemeyer, Robert A. (2003). Death anxiety and attitude toward the elderly among older adults: the role of gender and ethnicity. *Death Studies,* 27(4): 335-354.

Dhar, Upinder; Mehta, Savita; and Dhar, Santosh. (1998). Manual for Death Anxiety Scale. Agra: National Psychological Corporation.

Dictionary of Behavioral Science. (1973). New York: Van Nostrand Reinhold Company.

Downey, Ann M. (1984). Relationship of religiosity to Death Anxiety of Middle-aged Males. *Psychological Reports,* 54:811-822.

Dulark, Joseph A. (2002). Encyclopedia of Aging. New York: Quill.

Encarta World English Dictionary. (1999). Sydney: Pan Macmillan Australia Private Limited.

Ens, Carla and Bond, John B. (2007). Death anxiety in Adolescents: the contributions of bereavement and religiosity. *Omega,* 55(3): 169-184.

Fitz-Gibbon, Carol Taylor &Morris, Lynn Lyons. (1982). How to Calculate Statistics. Beverly Hills/ London: Sage Publications.

Freud, S. (1932). New Introductory Lectures on Psycho-Analysis, tr. by Sprott, W.J.H., Norton, New York, 1933.

Henry E. Garrett (1981). Statistics in Psychology and Education, 10th reprint. Bombay: Vakils Pfeffer and Simmons.

Henry E. Garrett (2007). Statistics in Psychology and Education, 12th reprint. Delhi: Paragon International Publishers.

Holocomb, R. N. (1975). Why Survive? Being Old in America. New York: Harper and Row.

Ireland, Mary. (1993). Death Anxiety and Self-Esteem in Children Four, Five and Six Years of Age: a Comparison of Minority Children who have AIDS with Minority Children who are healthy (Four-year-old, Five-year-old, Six-year-old Immune Deficiency). *Dissertation Abstracts International,* Vol. 56-01, Section: B, p.0172.

Kalish, R. A. & Reynolds, D. K. (1977). The role of age in death attitudes. *Death Education,* 1: 205-230.

Koocher, G. P., O'Malley, J. E., Foster, D., and Gogan, J. L. (1976). Death Anxiety in normal children and adolescents. *Psychiatria Clinica,* 9(3-4):220-229.

Kübler-Ross, E. (1969). On Death and Dying. New York: Macmillan.

Kübler-Ross, E. (1975). Death: The final stages of growth. New Jersey: Prentice Hall.

Langs, Robert. (1997). Death Anxiety and Clinical Practice. London: Karnac Books.

Lee, P. W., Lieh-Mak, F., Hung, B. K., and Luk, S. L. (1983-1984). Death Anxiety in Leukemic Chinese Children. *International Journal of Psychiatry Medicine,* 13(4): 281-289.

Lefton, L. A. (1982). Psychology, 2nd ed., U.S.A.: Allyn and Bacon.

Longman Dictionary of Psychology and Psychiatry (1984). New York: Longman.

Madnawat, A. V. Singh and Kachhawa, P. Singh. (2007). Age, Gender, and Living Circumstances: Discriminating Older Adults on Death Anxiety. *Death Studies,* 31: 763-769.

Mahabeer, M. and Bhana, K. (1984). The relationship between religion, religiosity and death anxiety among Indian adolescents. *South African Journal of Psychology,* 14:7-9.

McCarthy, J. B. (1980). Death Anxiety: The Loss of Self. USA: Gardner.

Niemeyer, R. A. and Niemeyer, G. J. (1984). Death Anxiety and counseling skill in the suicide interventionist. *Suicide & life-threatening behaviour,* 14(2):126-131.

Nutankumar, S. Thingujam and Ram, Usha. (2002). Death Anxiety among People of Peaceful and Disturbed Areas: A Comparative Study. *Paper presented at the National Conference on Yoga and Indian Approaches to Psychology. Pondicherry. India. September 29-October1, 2002.* Unpublished document.

Parsuram A. and Gandhi P. (1994). Beliefs and Death Anxiety. *Journal of the Indian Academy of Applied Psychology,* 20(2): 145-152.

Pierce Jr, John D., Cohen, Adam B., Chambers, Jacqueline A., and Meade, Rachel M. (2007). Gender Differences in death anxiety and religious orientation among US high school and college students. *Mental Health, Religion & Culture,* 10(2): 143-150.

Prakash, Col. Ved. (2008). Terrorism in India's North East: A Gathering Strom. Delhi: Kalpaz Publication. Vol. I & II.

Pratt, Clara Collette., Hare, Jan., and Wright, Cheryl. (1985). Death Anxiety and Comfort in teaching about death among preschool teachers. *Death Studies*, 9(5&6):417-425.

Raju, P. Mohan, (2009). Death anxiety among Ethiopian undergraduate students.

Rasmussen, C. A. and Brems, C. (1996). The relationship of Death Anxiety with age and psychological maturity. *The Journal of Psychology*, 130(2): 141-144.

Rattan, Anubhutti. (2005). the Question of Death and Death Anxiety, New York: Simon and Schuster.

Reigal, K. F. and Reigal, R. M. (1972). Development, drop and death. *Development Psychology*, 6:p.306-319.

Salter, C. A. & Salter, C. (1978). Death anxiety, attitudes and behaviour towards elderly of college students. *Gerontologist*, 16:232-236.

Saxene, N. R.; Mishra, B. K.; & Mohanty, R. K. (2004). Fundamentals of Educational Research, 4th ed., Meerut: R. Lall Book Depot.

Schumaker, J. F., Warren, W. G. and Groth-Marnat, G. (1991). Death Anxiety in Japan and Australia. *The Journal of Social Psychology*, 131(4): 511-518.

Sidhu, Kulbir Singh. (1984). Methodology of Educational Research. New Delhi: Sterling Publishers Pvt. Ltd.

Statistical Abstract Manipur. (2005). Directorate of Economics and Statistics, Government of Manipur.

Stedman's Medical Dictionary. 23rd ed. (1976). USA: The Williams and Wilkins Company.

Suhail, K. (2001). Death Anxiety in a Pakistani sample. *Journal of the Indian Academy of Applied Psychology*, 27(1-2): 19-27.

Suhail, Kausar and Akram, Saima. (2002). Correlates of Death Anxiety in Pakistan. *Death Studies*, 26(1): 39-50.

Suresh Singh, Rajkumar. (2013). Death Anxiety among Aged Manipuris, India. *ZENITH International Journal of Multidisciplinary Research*, 3(1): 209-216.

Tang, Catherine So-Kum.; Wu, Anise M.S.; and Yan, Elise C.W. (2002). Psychosocial Correlates of Death Anxiety Among Chinese College Students. *Death Studies*, 26:p.491-499.

Tate, L. A., (1982). Life Satisfaction and Death Anxiety in Aged Women. *International Journal of Aging & Human Development*, 15(4): 299-306.

The New International Webster's Dictionary and Thesaurus of the English Language (International Encyclopedic Edition). (2002).

Thorson, J. A. and Powell, F. C. (1988). Elements of Death Anxiety and Meanings of Death. *Journal of Clinical Psychology*, 44(5):691-701.

Thorson, J. A.; Powell, F. C. and Samuel, V. T. (1999). Age differences in death anxiety among African-American women. *Psychological reports*, 83(3 Pt. 2): 1173-1174.

Uppsala Conflict Data Programme (UCDP). (2008). International Data Base. http://www.ucdp.uu.se/ Accessed on March 15, 2010.

Webster's Dictionary (1980). Canada: Trident Press International.

APPENDIX A

OPINIONNAIRES

Death Anxiety among students: A case-study of Manipur University

Researcher:

Rajkumar Suresh Singh

M.A., M.Ed

UGC-NET/JRF (Adult Education & Education)

Dear Friend,

This scale consists of 10 (ten) statements having a choice of "Yes" or "No" against it. Please mark your response by putting a tick (✓) mark on the cell against each item. No answer is right or wrong. Respond the choice as per its applicability to you. Your response will be kept fully confidential. Though there is no time limit, you may finish as early as possible.

I hope you will surely co-operate and lend your helping hand for better finding.

Please fill-up your back-ground information:

NAME :..

AGE   : .... years   SEX : Male/Female

EDUCATIONALQUALIFICATION: ....

HOME ADDRESS: ....

RESPONSE SHEET

Death Anxiety among students: A case-study of Manipur University

Sl.	STATEMENT	YES	NO
1.	I do not like old age.		
2.	I am afraid of taking medicine given by a pharmacist without prescriptions.		
3.	I get panicky on even having a mild chest pain.		
4.	I can see a criminal being hanged.		
5.	I am not willing to see anybody dying.		
6.	I dread suffocating surrounding.		
7.	I get nervous on hearing about someone's sudden death.		
8.	I get frightened on seeing serious injuries in an accident.		
9.	I am not willing to die at anyplace other than home.		
10.	I get frightened on looking down from a height.		

Date: ..../........./ 2010   Signature:...........................